AF199006

Impressum
Verlag: BABADADA GmbH, Nedderfeld 112 , 22529 Hamburg
Geschäftsführer / Verlagsleitung: Harald Hof
Druck: Books on Demand GmbH, In de Tarpen 42, 22848 Norderstedt

Imprint
Publisher: BABADADA GmbH, Nedderfeld 112 , 22529 Hamburg, Germany
Managing Director / Publishing direction: Harald Hof
Print: Books on Demand GmbH, In de Tarpen 42, 22848 Norderstedt

school

مدرسه

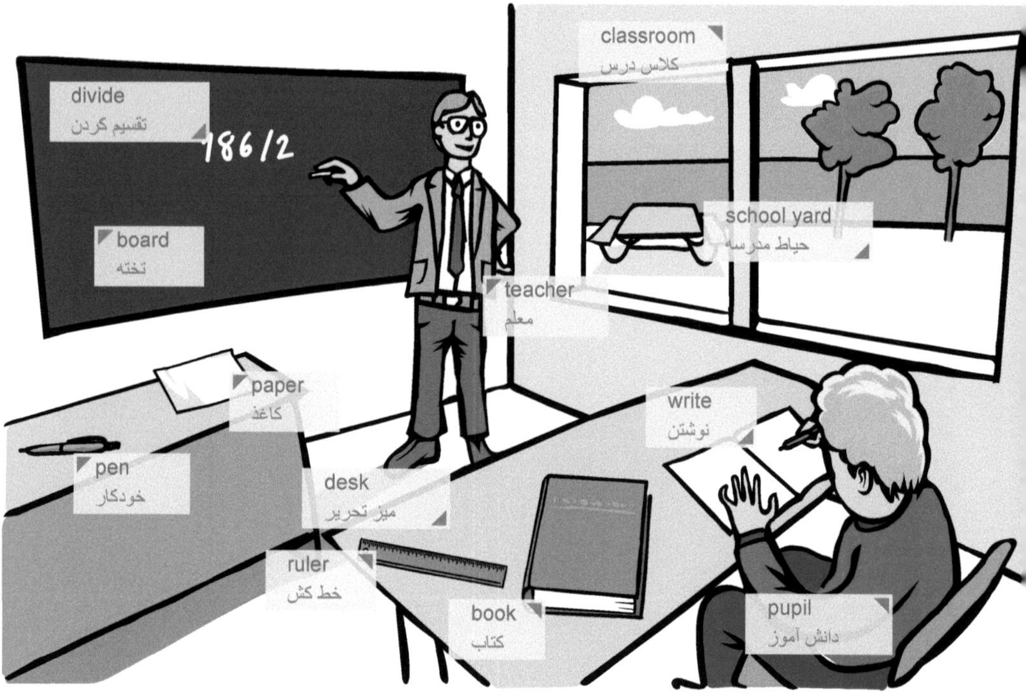

classroom
کلاس درس
divide
تقسیم کردن
186/2
board
تخته
school yard
حیاط مدرسه
teacher
معلم
paper
کاغذ
write
نوشتن
pen
خودکار
desk
میز تحریر
ruler
خط کش
book
کتاب
pupil
دانش آموز

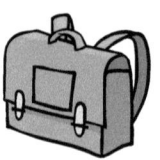

satchel
کیف مدرسه

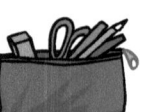

pencil case
جامدادی

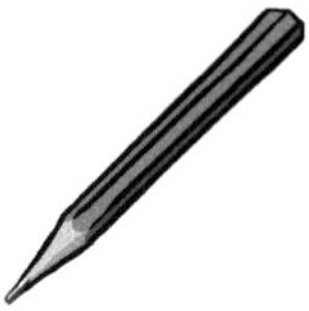

pencil
مداد

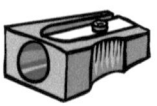

pencil sharpener
تراش

rubber
پاک کن

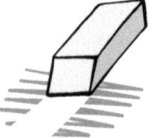

drawing pad
دفتر رسم

drawing

طراحی

paintbrush

قلم مو

paint box

جعبه ی آبرنگ

scissors

قیچی

glue

چسب

exercise book

کتاب تمرین

homework

تکلیف خانه

number

رقم

add

جمع کردن

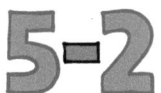

subtract

تفریقِ کردن

multiply

ضرب کردن

calculate

محاسبه کردن

letter

حرف الفبا

alphabet

الفبا

word

کلمه

text

متن

read

خواندن

chalk

گچ

lesson

درس

register

ثبت نام

examination

امتحان

certificate

مدرک رسمی

school uniform

لباس مدرسه

education

تحصیلات

encyclopedia

دانشنامه

university

دانشگاه

microscope

میکروسکوپ

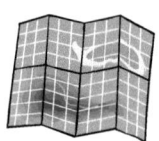

map

نقشه

waste-paper basket

سبد کاغذ باطله

travel
سفر

hotel
هتل
Grand
hostel
مسافرخانه
ROOMS
EXCHANGE
currency exchange office
صرافی
car
اتومبیل

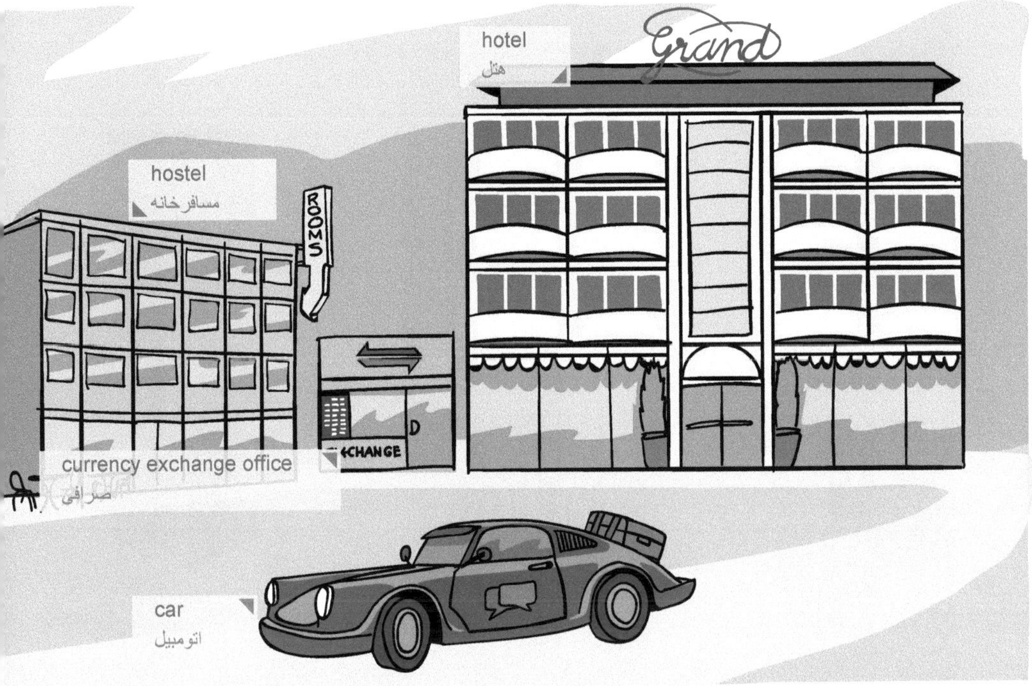

language

زبان

yes / no

بله / خیر

Okay

اُکی

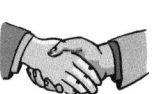

hello

سلام

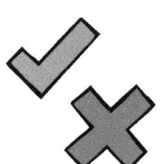

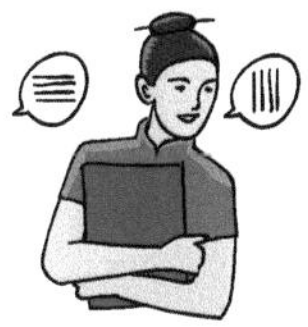

translator

مترجم

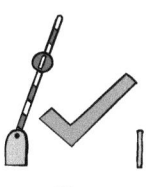

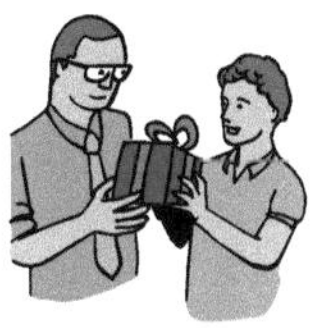

Thank you

ممنون

how much is...?

قیمت ... چه قدر است؟

I don´t get it

من متوجه نمی شوم

problem

مشکل

Good evening!

عصر بخیر! / شب بخیر!

Good morning!

صبح بخیر!

Good night!

شب بخیر!

goodbye

خدانگهدار

direction

جهت

luggage

بار سفر

bag

کیف

backpack

کوله پشتی

guest

مهمان

room

اتاق

sleeping bag

کیسه خواب

tent

خیمه

travel - سفر

tourist information

مرکز راهنمای گردشگران

beach

ساحل

credit card

کارت اعتباری

breakfast

صبحانه

lunch

نهار

dinner

شام

Ticket

بلیط

elevator

آسانسور

stamp

مهر

border

مرز

customs

گمرک

embassy

سفارتخانه

visa

ویزا

passport

گذرنامه

transport
حمل و نقل

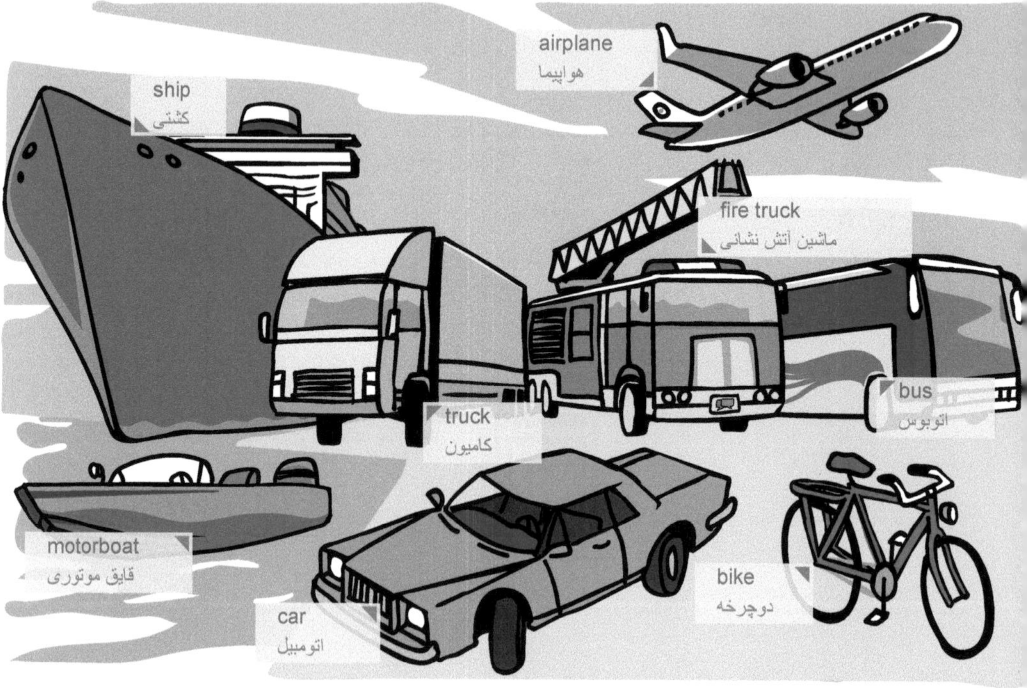
airplane
هواپیما
ship
کشتی
fire truck
ماشین آتش نشانی
bus
اتوبوس
truck
کامیون
motorboat
قایق موتوری
bike
دوچرخه
car
اتومبیل

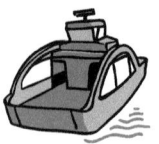

ferry
کشتی مسافربری

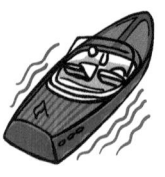

boat
قایق

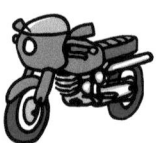

motorbike
موتورسیکلت

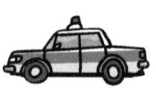

police car
ماشین پلیس

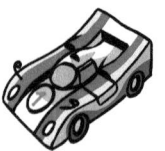

racing car
ماشین مسابقه

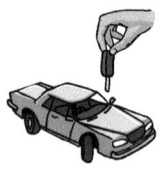

rental car
ماشین کرایه ای

car sharing

به اشتراک گذاری اتوموبیل

tow truck

جرثقیل

garbage truck

ماشین حمل زباله

engine

موتور

fuel

بنزین

fuel station

پمپ بنزین

traffic sign

تابلو راهنمایی و رانندگی

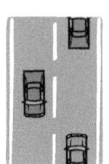

traffic

عبور و مرور

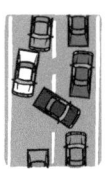

traffic jam

ترافیک

parking lot

پارکینگ

train station

ایستگاه قطار

tracks

ریل راه آهن

train

قطار

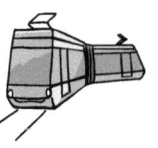

tram

قطار برقی

wagon

واگن

helicopter

هلیکوپتر

airport

فرودگاه

tower

برج

passenger

مسافر

container

کانتینر

carton

کارتن

cart

گاری

basket

سبد

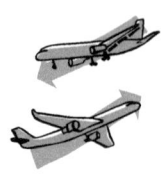

take off / land

به پرواز درآمدن / فرود آمدن

city

شهر

village

دهکده

city center

مرکز شهر

house

خانه

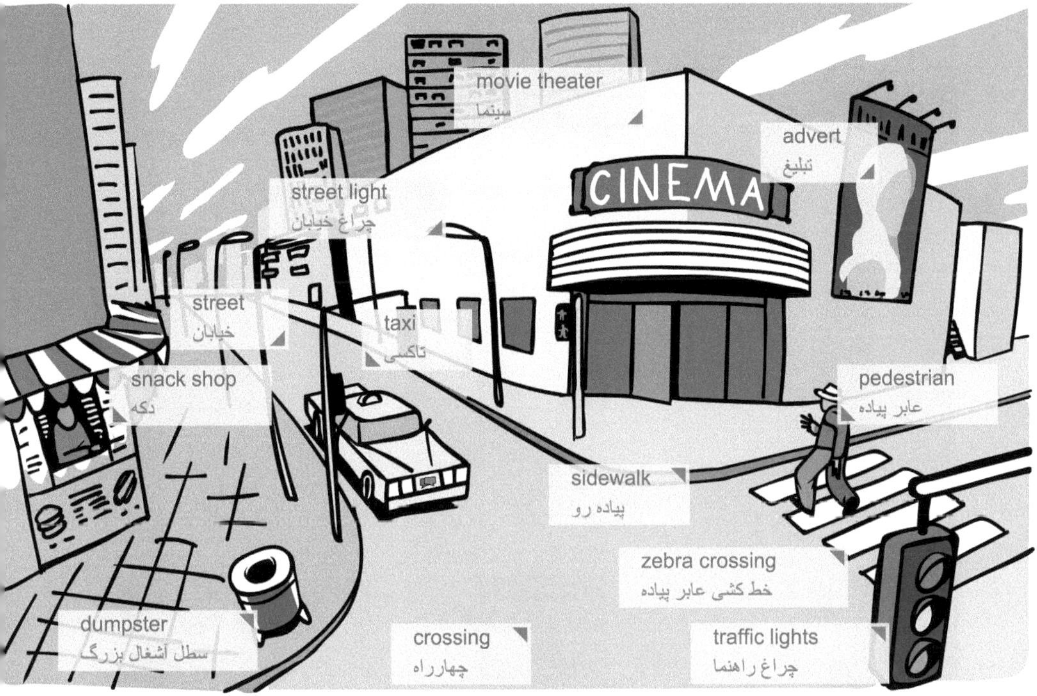

movie theater
سینما

advert
تبلیغ

street light
چراغ خیابان

street
خیابان

taxi
تاکسی

CINEMA

snack shop
دکه

pedestrian
عابر پیاده

sidewalk
پیاده رو

zebra crossing
خط کشی عابر پیاده

dumpster
سطل آشغال بزرگ

crossing
چهارراه

traffic lights
چراغ راهنما

hut
کلبه

apartment
آپارتمان

train station
ایستگاه قطار

city hall
ساختمان شهرداری

museum
موزه

school
مدرسه

university

دانشگاه

bank

بانک

hospital

بیمارستان

hotel

هتل

pharmacy

داروخانه

office

اداره

book shop

کتابفروشی

shop

مغازه

flower shop

گل فروشی

supermarket

سوپرمارکت

market

بازار

department store

فروشگاه بزرگ

fishmonger's shop

ماهی فروش

mall

مرکز خرید

harbor

بندر

park

پارک

bench

نیمکت

bridge

پل

stairs

پله

subway

مترو

tunnel

تونل

bus stop

ایستگاه اتوبوس

bar

میخانه

restaurant

رستوران

postbox

صندوق پست

street sign

تابلوی خیابان

parking meter

دستگاه پارکومتر

zoo

باغ وحش

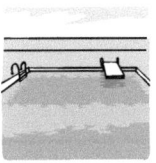

swimming pool

استخر شنای عمومی

mosque

مسجد

farm

مزرعه

pollution

آلودگی محیط زیست

cemetery

قبرستان

church

کلیسا

playground

زمین بازی

temple

معبد

landscape

چشم انداز

signpost
تابلوی راهنمای مسیر

path
راه

meadow
چمنزار

stone
سنگ

tree
درخت

hiker
راه نورد

river
رودخانه

grass
چمن

flower
گل

valley

دره

hill

تپه

lake

دریاچه

forest

جنگل

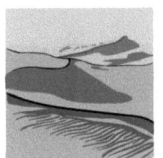

desert

بیابان

volcano

کوه آتشفشان

castle

قلعه

rainbow

رنگین کمان

mushroom

قارچ

palm tree

درخت نخل

mosquito

پشه

fly

مگس

ant

مورچه

bee

زنبور

spider

عنکبوت

beetle

سوسک

frog

قورباغه

squirrel

سنجاب

hedgehog

جوجه تیغی

hare

خرگوش صحرایی

owl

جغد

bird

پرنده

swan

قو

boar

گراز

deer

گوزن نر

moose

گوزن شمالی

dam

سد آب

wind turbine

توربین بادی

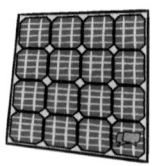

solar panel

صفحه ی خورشیدی

climate

آب و هوا

restaurant
رستوران

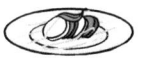

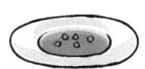

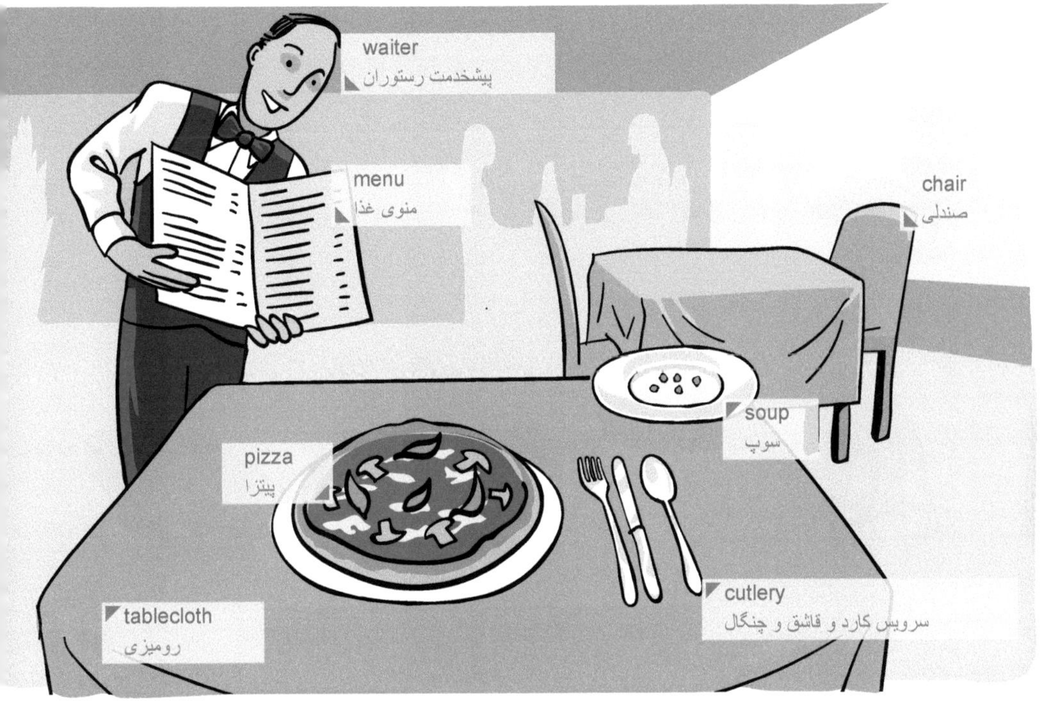

waiter
پیشخدمت رستوران
menu
منوی غذا
chair
صندلی
soup
سوپ
pizza
پیتزا
cutlery
سرویس کارد و قاشق و چنگال
tablecloth
رومیزی

starter
....
پیش‌غذا

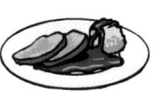

main course
....
غذای اصلی

dessert
....
دسر

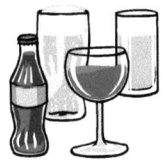

drinks
....
نوشیدنی ها

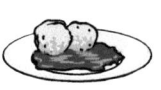

food
....
غذا

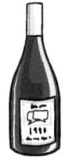

bottle
....
بطری

fast food

فست فود

street food

اغذیه خیابانی

teapot

قوری

sugar bowl

قندان

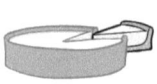

portion

پُرس غذا

espresso machine

دستگاه اسپرسو

high chair

صندلی پایه بلند غذاخوری بچه

bill

صورتحساب

tray

سینی

knife

چاقو

fork

چنگال

spoon

قاشق

teaspoon

قاشق چایخوری

serviette

دستمال سفره

glass

لیوان

plate

بشقاب

soup plate

بشقاب سوپخوری

saucer

نعلبکی

sauce

سس

salt shaker

نمکدان

pepper mill

فلفل ساب

vinegar

سرکه

oil

روغن خوراکی

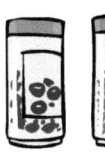

spices

ادویه جات

ketchup

سس کچاپ

mustard

سس خردل

mayonnaise

سس مایونز

supermarket

سوپرمارکت

special offer
پیشنهاد ویژه
FOR
customer
مشتری
dairy products
لبنیات
fruit
میوه جات
shopping cart
چرخ دستی خرید

BUTCHERS

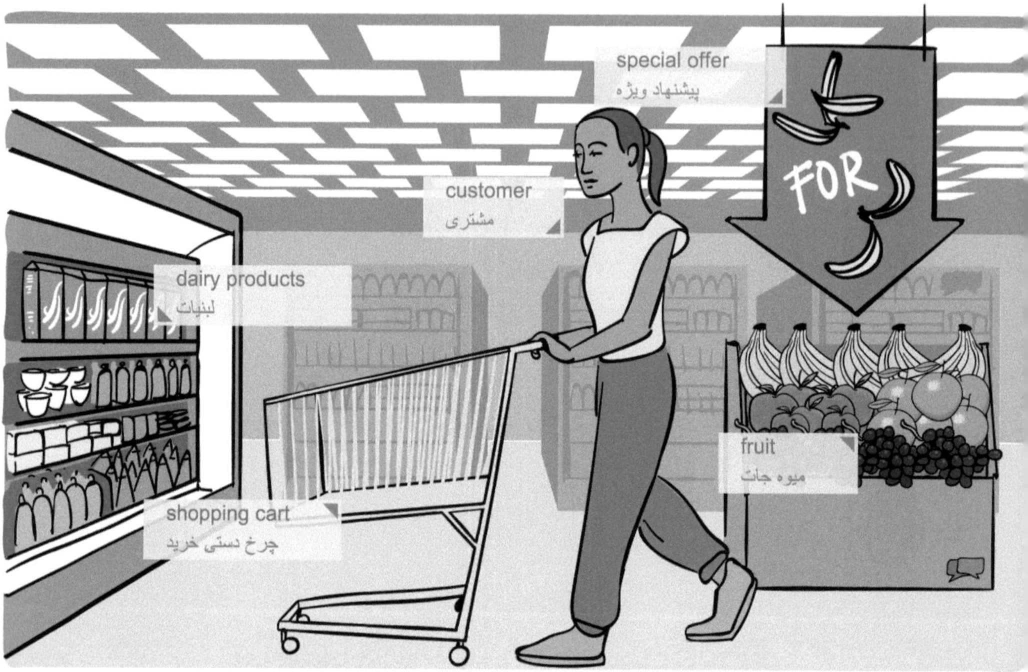

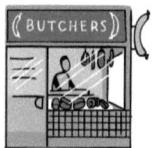

butcher's shop
....
قصابی

BAKERY

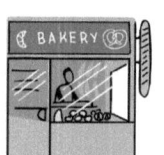

bakery
....
نانوایی

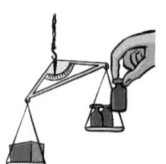

weigh
....
وزن کردن

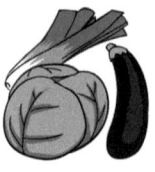

vegetables
....
سبزیجات

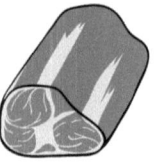

meat
....
گوشت

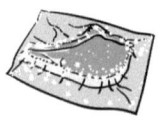

frozen food
....
غذای منجمد

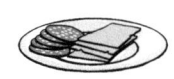

cold cuts

مخلوطی از انواع کالباس یا پنیر که
ورقه ای بریده شده باشند

canned food

غذای کنسروی

detergent

پودر لباسشویی

candy

شیرینی جات

household products

لوازم خانگی

cleaning products

ماده شوینده و پاک کننده

sales representative

فروشنده

cash register

صندوق پرداخت

cashier

صندوقدار

shopping list

لیست خرید

opening hours

ساعات کار

wallet

کیف پول

credit card

کارت اعتباری

bag

کیف

plastic bag

کیسه ی پلاستیکی

water

آب

juice

آبمیوه

milk

شیر

coke

نوشابه کوکاکولا

wine

شراب

beer

آبجو

alcohol

الکل

cocoa

کاکائو

tea

چای

coffee

قهوه

espresso

قهوه اسپرسو

cappuccino

کاپوچینو

banana

موز

apple

سیب

orange

پرتقال

melon

انواع هندوانه و خربزه

lemon

لیمو

carrot

هویج

garlic

سیر

bamboo

نی بامبو

onion

پیاز

mushroom

قارچ

nuts

آجیل

noodles

ماکارونی

spaghetti

اسپاگتی

rice

برنج

salad

سالاد

fries

سیب زمینی سرخ کرده

fried potatoes

سیب زمینی سرخ شده

pizza

پیتزا

hamburger

همبرگر

sandwich

ساندویچ

escalope

شنیتسل

ham

ژامبون خوک

salami

سالامی

sausage

سوسیس

chicken

مرغ

roast

نوعی گوشت سرخ شده

fish

ماهی

porridge oats

جوی پرک شده

muesli

نوعی صبحانه مخلوطی از برگه ذرت و
میوه های خشک شده و خشکبار که
معمولا با شیر خورده می شود

cornflakes

کورنفلکس

flour

آرد

croissant

کرواسان

bread roll

نان بروتشن

bread

نان

toast

نان تست

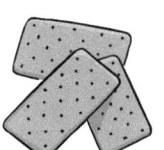

cookies

بیسکویت

butter

کره

curd

کشک

cake

کیک

egg

تخم مرغ

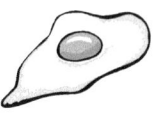

fried egg

تخم مرغ نیمرو

cheese

پنیر

ice cream

بستنی

sugar

شکر

honey

عسل

jelly

مربا

nougat cream

کرم شکلاتی بادامی

curry

ادویه کاری

farm
مزرعه

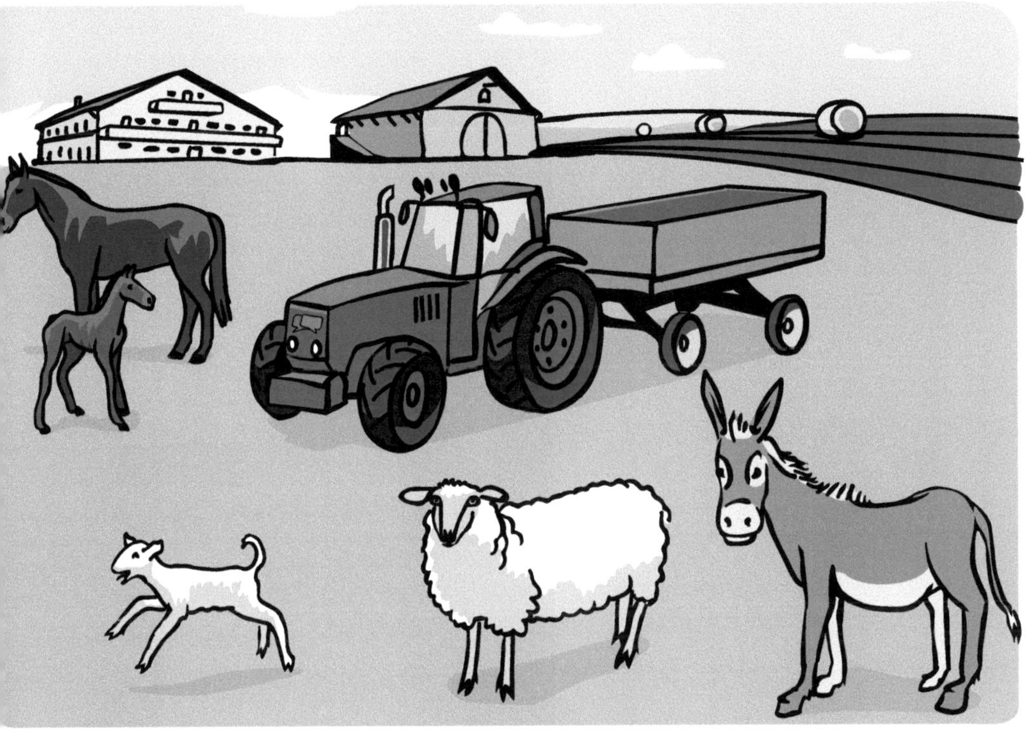

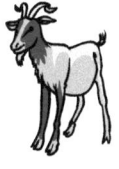

goat

بز

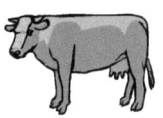

cow

گاو ماده

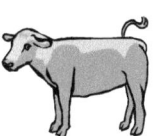

calf

گوساله

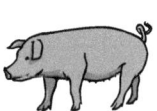

pig

خوک

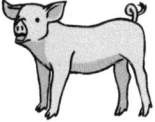

piglet

بچه خوک

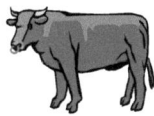

bull

گاو نر

goose

غاز

duck

اردک

chick

جوجه

hen

مرغ

cockerel

خروس

rat

موش صحرایی

cat

گربه

mouse

موش

ox

گاو نر اخته

dog

سگ

dog house

لانه ی سگ

garden hose

شلنگ باغبانی

watering can

آبپاش

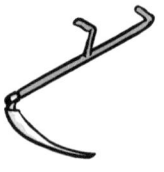

scythe

داس دسته بلند

plow

گاو آهن

sickle

داس

hoe

کج بیل

pitchfork

چنگک باغبانی

axe

تبر

pushcart

فرقون

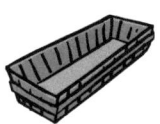

trough

آبشخور

milk can

بطری نگهداری شیر

sack

کیسه

fence

حصار

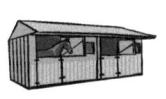

stable

اصطبل

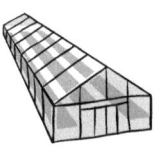

greenhouse

گلخانه

soil

خاک

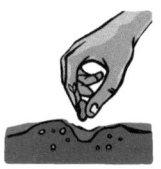

seed

بذر

fertilizer

کود

combine harvester

ماشین کمباین

harvest

برداشت کردن محصول

harvest

محصول

yams

تمیس

wheat

گندم

soya

سویا

potato

سیب زمینی

corn

ذرت

rapeseed

کلزا

fruit tree

درخت میوه

manioc

گیاه مانیوک

grain

غلات

living room

اتاق نشیمن

bathroom

حمام

kitchen

آشپزخانه

bedroom

اتاق خواب

kids room

اتاق بچه

dining room

ناهارخوری

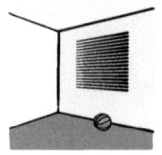

floor

کف زمین

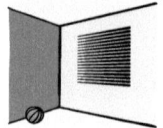

wall

دیوار

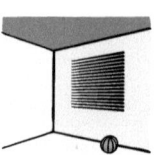

ceiling

سقف

cellar

زیرزمین

sauna

سونا

balcony

بالکن

terrace

تراس

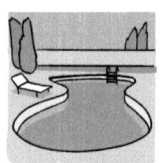

pool

استخر

lawn mower

ماشین چمن‌زنی

sheet

ملافه

bedspread

روتختی

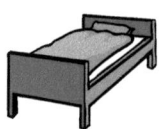

bed

تخت خواب

broom

جارو

bucket

سطل

switch

سوییچ یا کلید

living room
اتاق نشیمن

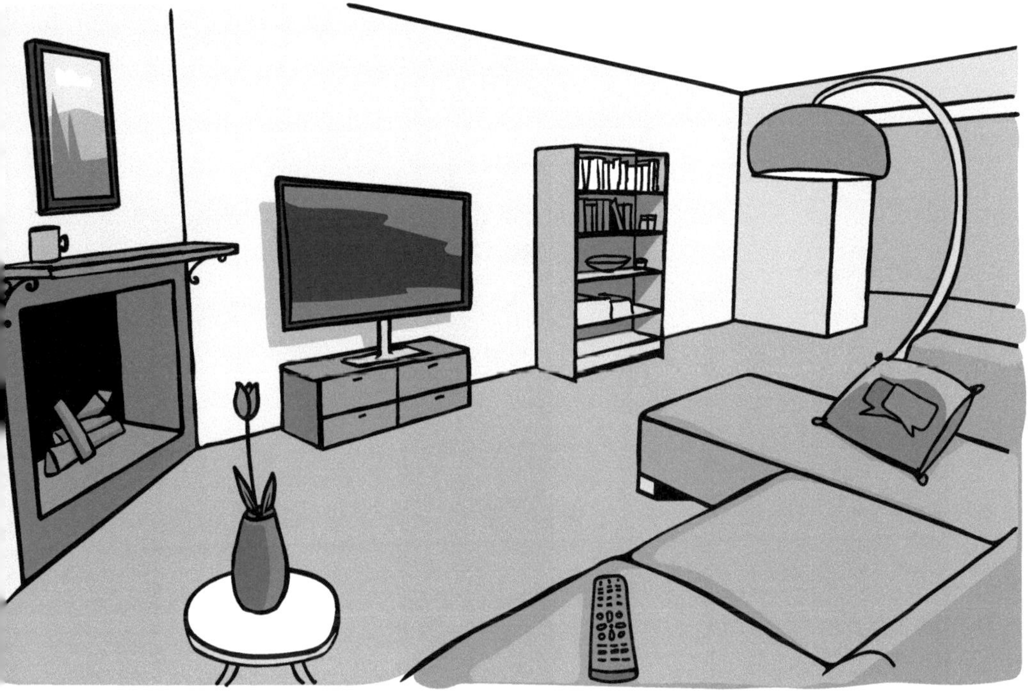

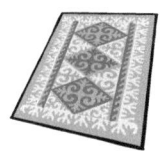

carpet

فرش

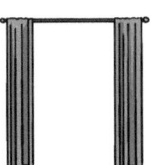

drape

پرده

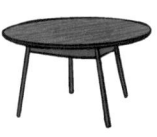

table

میز

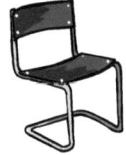

chair

صندلی

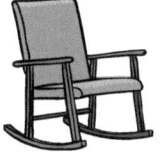

rocking chair

صندلی گهواره ایی

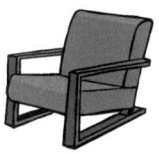

armchair

صندلی راحتی

book

كتاب

blanket

لحاف

decoration

دكوراسيون

firewood

هیزم

film

فیلم

stereo system

دستگاه ضبط صوت

key

کلید

newspaper

روزنامه

painting

تابلو نقاشی

poster

پوستر

radio

رادیو

notebook

دفترچه یادداشت

vacuum cleaner

جاروبرقی

cactus

کاکتوس

candle

شمع

kitchen
آشپزخانه

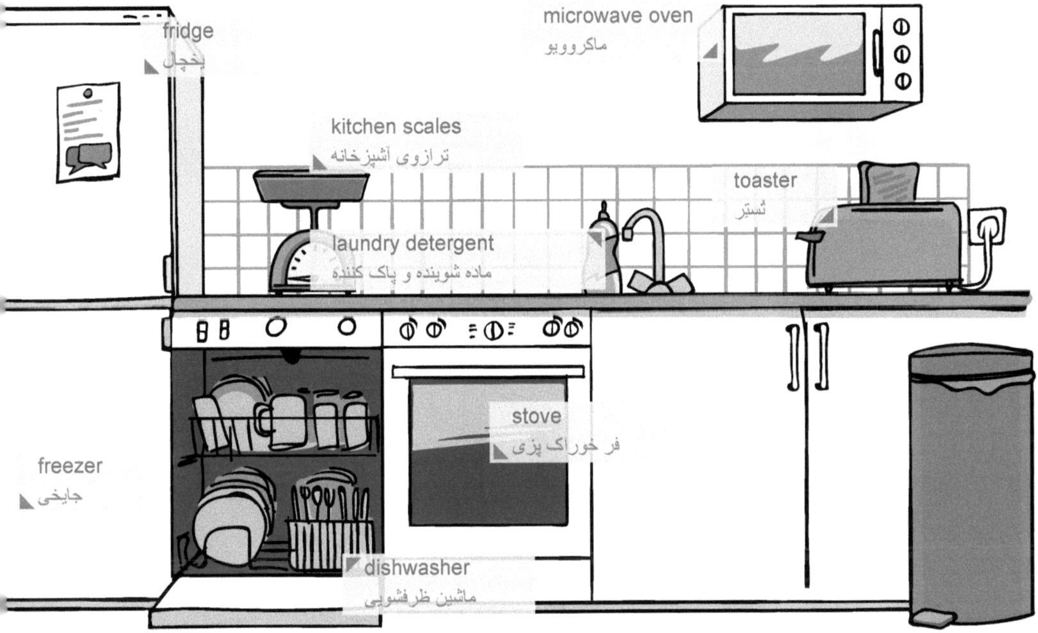
fridge
یخچال
microwave oven
ماکروویو
kitchen scales
ترازوی آشپزخانه
toaster
تُستر
laundry detergent
ماده شوینده و پاک کننده
stove
فر خوراک پزی
freezer
جایخی
dishwasher
ماشین ظرفشویی

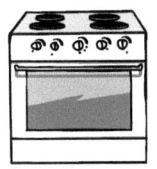

cooker
اجاق گاز

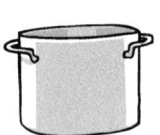

pot
قابلمه

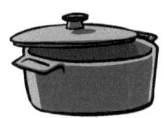

cast-iron pot
قابلمه چدنی

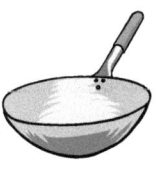

wok / kadai
ماهی تابه گود

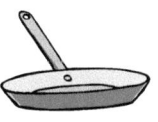

pan
ماهی تابه

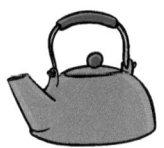

kettle
کتری

steamer

بخارپز

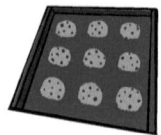

baking tray

سینی فر

crockery

ظرف چینی آشپزخانه

mug

لیوان

bowl

کاسه

chopsticks

چاپستیک

ladle

ملاقه

spatula

کفگیر

whisk

همزن

strainer

آبکش

sieve

آبکش

grater

رنده

mortar

هاون

barbecue

باربیکیو

fireplace

محل مخصوص افروختن آتش

chopping board

تخته گوشت و سبزی

rolling pin

وردنه

corkscrew

در بطری بازکن

can

قوطی

can opener

در قوطی بازکن

oven cloth

دستگیره پارچه ای

sink

سینک ظرفشویی

brush

برس گردگیری

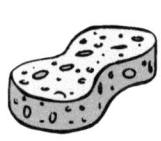

sponge

اسفنج

blender

مخلوط کن

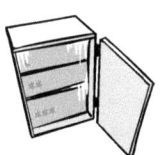

deep freezer

فریزر

baby bottle

شیشه شیر بچه

tap

شیر آب

bathroom

حمام

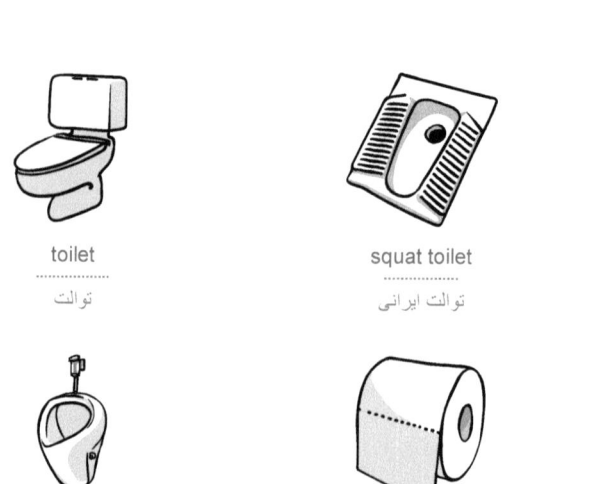

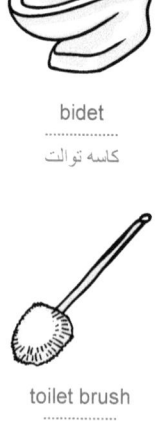

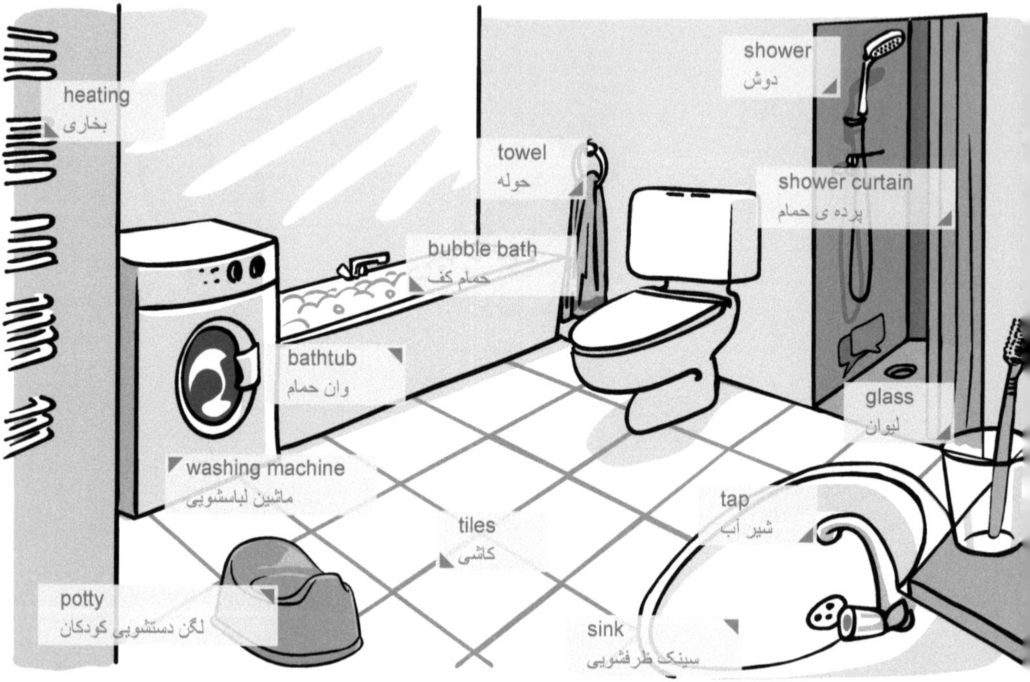
heating
بخاری
towel
حوله
shower
دوش
shower curtain
پرده ی حمام
bubble bath
حمام کف
bathtub
وان حمام
glass
لیوان
washing machine
ماشین لباسشویی
tap
شیر آب
tiles
کاشی
potty
لگن دستشویی کودکان
sink
سینک ظرفشویی

toilet

توالت

squat toilet

توالت ایرانی

bidet

کاسه توالت

urinal

توالت مخصوص آقایان

toilet paper

دستمال توالت

toilet brush

فرچه توالت

toothbrush

مسواک

toothpaste

خمیردندان

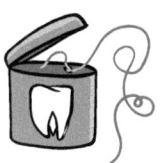

dental floss

نخ دندان

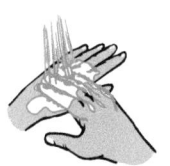

wash

شستن

hand shower

دوش آب تلفنی

douche

شلنگ توالت

basin

لگن روشویی

back brush

برس شست و شوی پشت

soap

صابون

shower gel

شامپو بدن

shampoo

شامپو

flannel

لیف حمام

drain

راه آب

creme

کرم

deodorant

اسپری دئودورانت

mirror

آیینه

hand mirror

آیینه ی کوچک دستی

razor

تیغ ریش تراشی

shaving foam

کف ریش تراشی

aftershave

آفترشیو

comb

شانه ی سر

brush

برس

hair-dryer

سشوار

hairspray

اسپری مو

makeup

أرایش

lipstick

رژلب

nail varnish

لاک ناخن

cotton wool

پنبه

nail scissors

قیچی ناخن

perfume

عطر

washbag

کیف لوازم آرایشی و بهداشتی

stool

چهارپایه

weighing scales

ترازو

bathrobe

حوله ی، بالتویی

rubber gloves

دستکش ظرفشویی

tampon

تامپون

sanitary towel

نوار بهداشتی

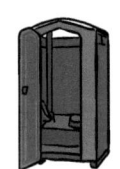

chemical toilet

توالت سیار

kids room

اتاق بچه

alarm clock
ساعت زنگدار
cuddly toy
نوعی عروسک نرم به شکل حیوانات
toy car
ماشین اسباب بازی
rattle
جغجغه
doll's house
خانه ی عروسکی
present
کادو

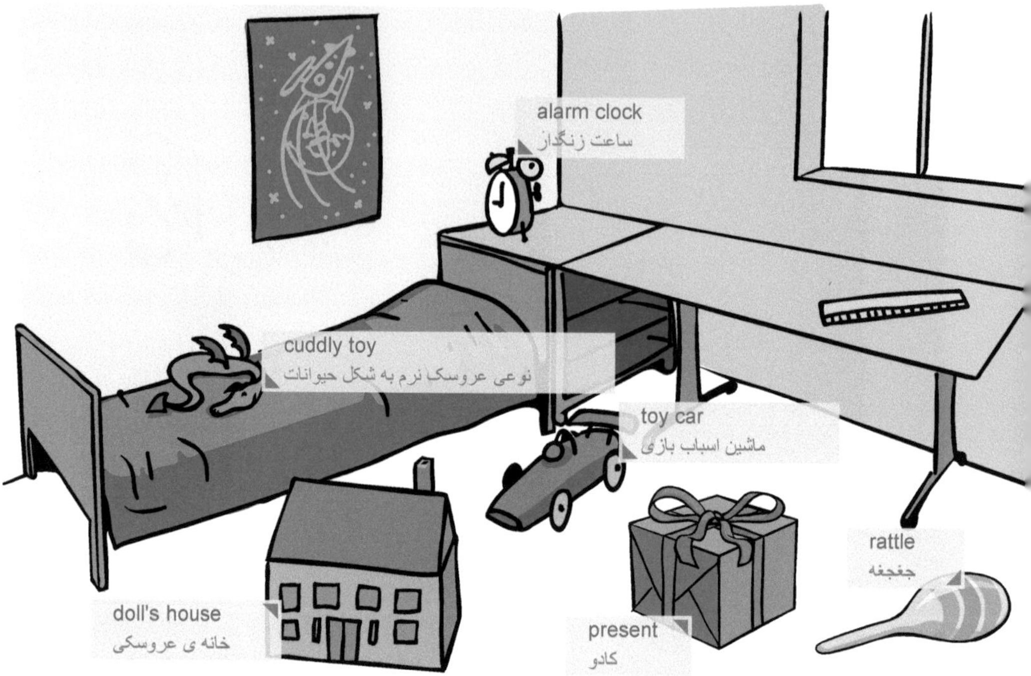

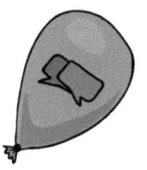

balloon
بادکنک

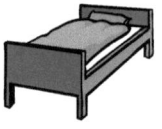

bed
تخت خواب

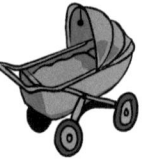

stroller
کالسکه بچه

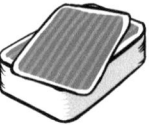

deck of cards
بازی ورق

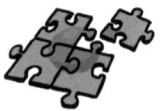

jigsaw
پازل

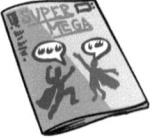

comic
داستان مصور

lego bricks

اسباب بازی لگو

toy blocks

خانه سازی

action figure

عروسک شخصیت های فیلم و کارتون

romper suit

لباس نوزاد

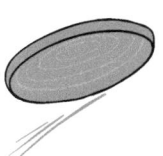

frisbee

فریزبی

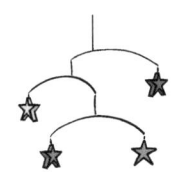

mobile

نوعی اسباب بازی که روی تخت نوزاد یا کودک نصب می شود

board game

بازی روی صفحه

dice

تاس

model train set

قطار اسباب بازی

pacifier

پستانک

party

مهمانی

picture book

کتاب مصور

ball

توپ

doll

عروسک

play

بازی کردن

sandpit

جعبه شنی مخصوص بازی کودکان

swing

تاب

toys

اسباب بازی

video game console

کنسول بازی های کامپیوتری

tricycle

سه چرخه

teddy bear

خرس عروسکی

wardrobe

کمد لباس

clothing

لباس

socks

جوراب

stockings

جوراب زنانه ساق بلند

tights

جوراب شلواری

scarf
شال

umbrella
چتر

t-shirt
تی شرت

belt
کمربند

boots
پوتین

slippers
دمپایی

sneakers
کفش ورزشی کتانی

sandals
صندل

shoes
کفش

rubber boots
چکمه پلاستیکی

underwear
شرت

bra
سوتین

undershirt
جلیقه

clothing - لباس   45

body

بادی

pants

شلوار

jeans

جین

skirt

دامن

blouse

بلوز

shirt

پیراهن

pullover

پولیور

sweater

سویی شرت

blazer

نوعی کت

jacket

ژاکت

coat

کت بلند

raincoat

بارانی

costume

لباس نمایش

dress

لباس

wedding dress

لباس عروس

suit

كت و شلوار

nightgown

لباس خواب زنانه

pajamas

پیژامه

sari

ساری،

headscarf

روسری

turban

دستمال

burka

برقع

kaftan

قبا

abaya

عبا

swimsuit

لباس شنا

trunks

شرت شنا

shorts

شلوارک

tracksuit

لباس ورزشی

apron

پیشبند

gloves

دستکش

button

دکمه

glasses

عینک

bracelet

دستبند

necklace

گردنبند

ring

انگشتر

earring

گوشواره

cap

کلاه لبه دار

coat hanger

چوب لباسی

hat

کلاه

tie

کراوات

zip

زیپ

helmet

کلاه ایمنی

braces

بند شلوار

school uniform

لباس مدرسه

uniform

لباس فرم

bib

پیش بند بچه

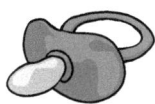

pacifier

پستانک

diaper

پوشک بچه

office

اداره

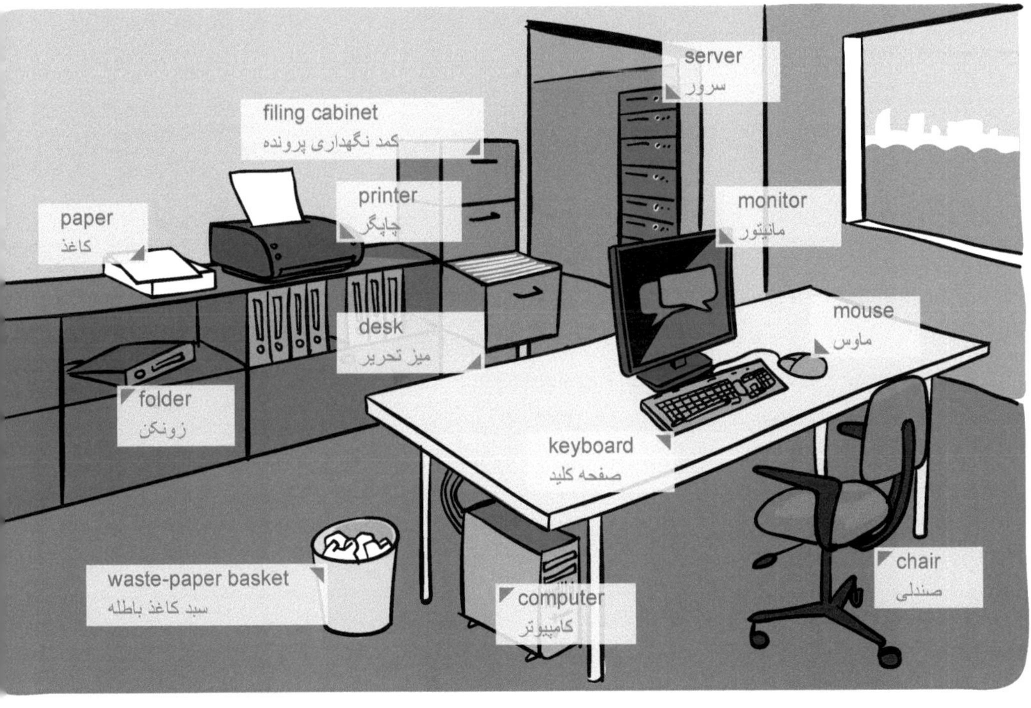

server

سرور

filing cabinet

کمد نگهداری پرونده

printer

چاپگر

monitor

مانیتور

paper

کاغذ

mouse

ماوس

desk

میز تحریر

folder

زونکن

keyboard

صفحه کلید

chair

صندلی

waste-paper basket

سبد کاغذ باطله

computer

کامپیوتر

coffee mug

لیوان قهوه

calculator

ماشین حساب

internet

اینترنت

laptop

لپ تاپ

letter

نامه

message

پیغام

cell phone

تلفن همراه

network

شبکه ی ارتباطی

photocopier

دستگاه فتوکپی

software

نرم افزار

telephone

تلفن

plug socket

پریز

fax machine

دستگاه فاکس

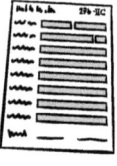

form

فرم

document

مدرک

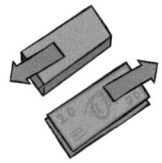

buy

خريدن

pay

پرداخت کردن

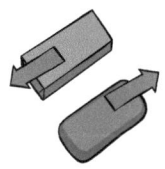

trade

تجارت کردن

money

پول

dollar

دلار

euro

يورو

yen

ين

rouble

روبل

Swiss franc

فرانک سوئیس

renminbi yuan

یوان رنمینبی

rupee

روپیه

cash point

دستگاه خودپرداز

currency exchange office

صرافی

gold

طلا

silver

نقره

oil

نفت

energy

انرژی

price

قیمت

contract

قرارداد

tax

مالیات

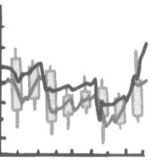

stock

سهام سرمایه

work

کار کردن

employee

کارمند

employer

کارفرما

factory

کارخانه

shop

مغازه

police officer

مامور پلیس

fireman

آتش نشان

cook

آشپز

doctor

دکتر

pilot

خلبان

gardener

باغبان

carpenter

نجار

seamstress

خیاط زنانه

judge

قاضی

chemist

شیمیدان

actor

بازیگر

bus driver

راننده اتوبوس

taxi driver

راننده تاکسی

fisherman

ماهیگیر

cleaning lady

نظافتچی زن

roofer

سقف ساز

waiter

پیشخدمت رستوران

hunter

شکارچی

painter

نقاش

baker

نانوا

electrician

برقکار

builder

کارگر ساختمانی

engineer

مهندس

butcher

قصاب

plumber

لوله کش

postman

پستچی

soldier

سرباز

architect

معمار

cashier

صندوقدار

florist

گل فروش

hairdresser

آرایشگر

conductor

مامور کنترل بلیط در قطار

mechanic

مکانیک

captain

ناخدا

dentist

دندانپزشک

scientist

دانشمند

rabbi

عالم یهودی

imam

امام

monk

راهب

pastor

کشیش

tools
ابزارآلات

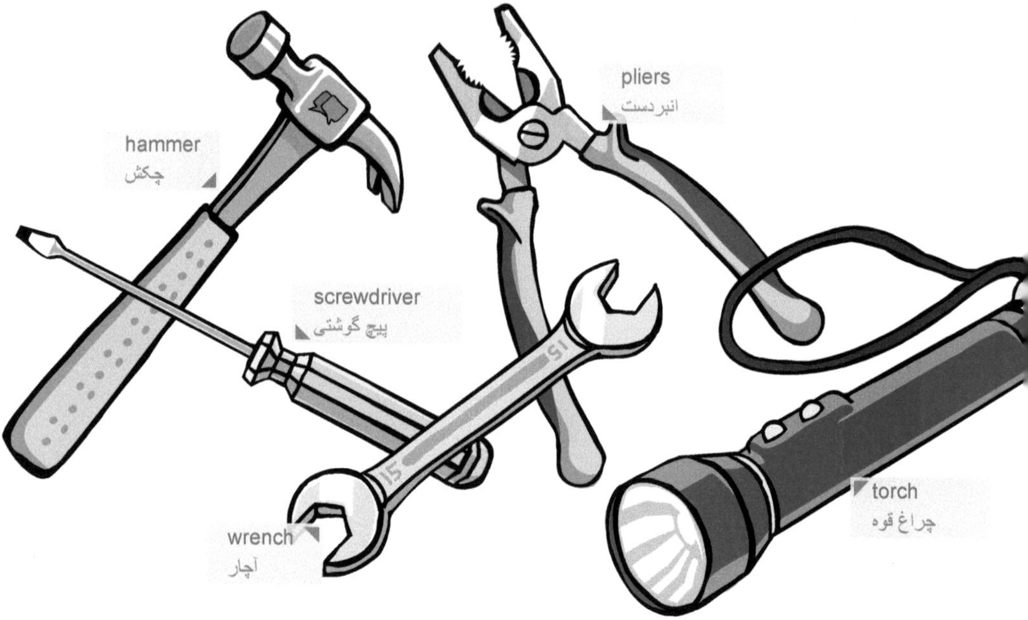

pliers
انبردست
hammer
چکش
screwdriver
پیچ گوشتی
torch
چراغ قوه
wrench
آچار

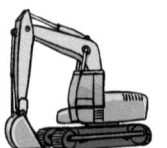

excavator
بیل مکانیکی

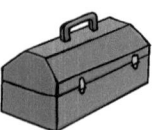

toolbox
جعبه ابزار

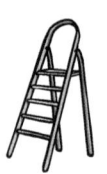

ladder
نردبان

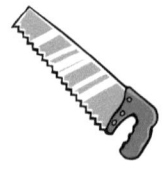

saw
ارّه

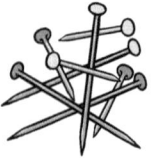

nails
میخ

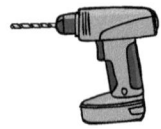

drill
مته

repair

تعمیر کردن

shovel

بیل

Damn!

لعنتی!

dustpan

خاک انداز

paint can

سطل رنگرزی

screws

پیچ

musical instruments

آلات موسیقی

loud speaker
بلندگو

drum set
درامز

guitar
گیتار

double bass
کنترباس

trumpet
ترومپت

piano

پیانو

violin

ویولن

bass

گیتار بیس

timpani

تیمپانی

drums

طبل

keyboard

کیبورد الکتریک

saxophone

ساکسیفون

flute

فلوت

microphone

میکروفون

باغ وحش

tiger
ببر

entrance
ورودی

cage
قفس

zebra
گورخر

animal feed
خوراک حیوانات

panda
خرس پاندا

animals

حیوانات

elephant

فیل

kangaroo

کانگورو

rhino

کرگدن

gorilla

گوریل

bear

خرس

camel

شتر

ostrich

شترمرغ

lion

شیر

monkey

میمون

flamingo

فلامینگو

parrot

طوطی

polar bear

خرس قطبی

penguin

پنگوئن

shark

کوسه

peacock

طاووس

snake

مار

crocodile

تمساح

zookeeper

نگهبان باغ وحش

seal

خوک آبی

jaguar

پلنگ امریکایی

pony

اسب کوچک

leopard

پلنگ

hippo

اسب آبی

giraffe

زرافه

eagle

عقاب

boar

گراز

fish

ماهی

turtle

لاک پشت

walrus

شیرماهی

fox

روباه

gazelle

غزال

American football
فوتبال آمریکایی

cycling
دوچرخه سواری

tennis
تنیس

basketball
بسکتبال

swimming
شنا

boxing
بوکس

ice hockey
هاکی روی یخ

soccer

فوتبال

badminton

بدمینتون

athletics

دوومیدانی

handball

هندبال

skiing

اسکی

polo

پولو

jump
پریدن

laugh
خندیدن

hug
بغل کردن

walk
راه رفتن

sing
آواز خواندن

pray
دعا کردن

kiss
بوسیدن

dream
رؤیا دیدن

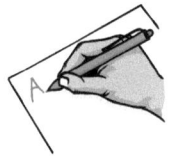

write

نوشتن

draw

رسم کردن

show

نشان دادن

push

هل دادن

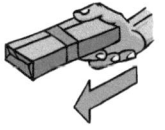

give

دادن

take

برداشتن

have

داشتن

do

انجام دادن

be

بودن

stand

ایستادن

run

دویدن

pull

کشیدن

throw

پرتاب کردن

fall

افتادن

lie

دراز کشیدن

wait

منتظر بودن

carry

حمل کردن

sit

نشستن

get dressed

لباس پوشیدن

sleep

خوابیدن

wake up

بیدار شدن

look at

تماشا کردن

cry

گریه کردن

stroke

نوازش کردن

comb

شانه کردن

talk

حرف زدن

understand

فهمیدن

ask

پرسیدن

listen

شنیدن

drink

آشامیدن

eat

خوردن

tidy up

مرتب کردن

love

عاشق بودن

cook

پختن

drive

رانندگی کردن

fly

پرواز کردن

sail

قایقرانی کردن

calculate

محاسبه کردن

read

خواندن

learn

یاد گرفتن

work

کار کردن

marry

ازدواج کردن

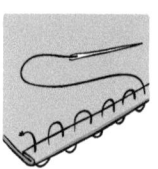

sew

دوختن

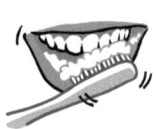

brush teeth

مسواک زدن

kill

کشتن

smoke

سیگار کشیدن

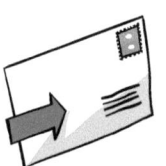

send

فرستادن

family
خانواده

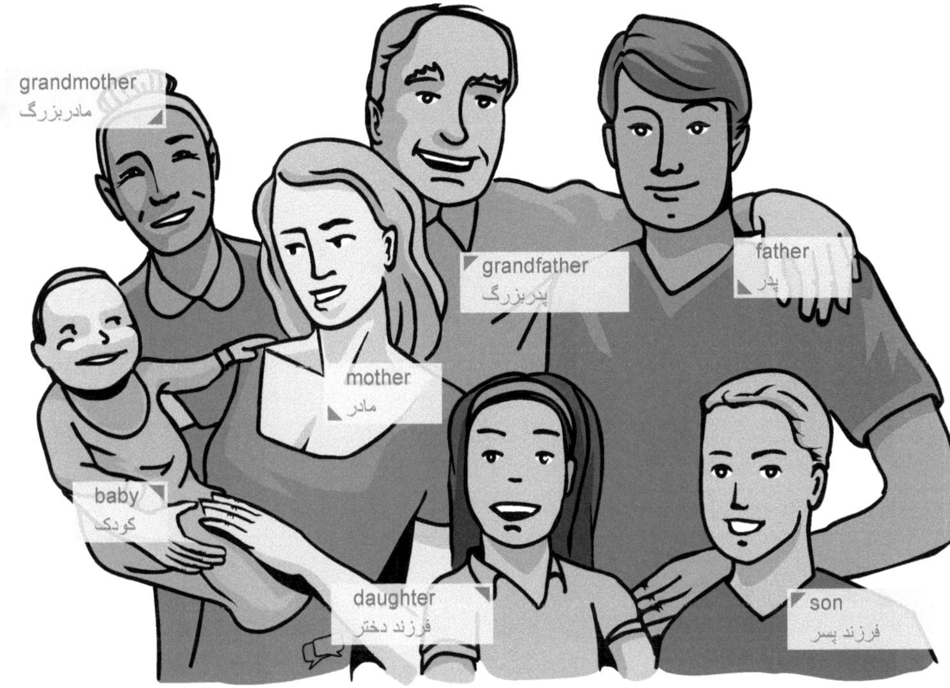
grandmother
مادربزرگ
grandfather
پدربزرگ
father
پدر
mother
مادر
baby
کودک
daughter
فرزند دختر
son
فرزند پسر

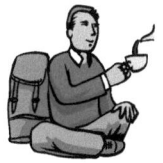

guest

مهمان

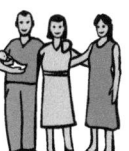

aunt

خاله، عمه

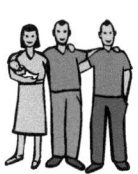

uncle

دایی، عمو

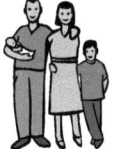

brother

برادر

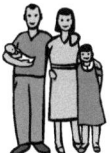

sister

خواهر

body

بدن

forehead
پیشانی
eye
چشم
shoulder
شانه
finger
انگشت دست
face
صورت
chin
چانه
hand
دست
leg
ساق پا
breast
سینه
arm
بازو

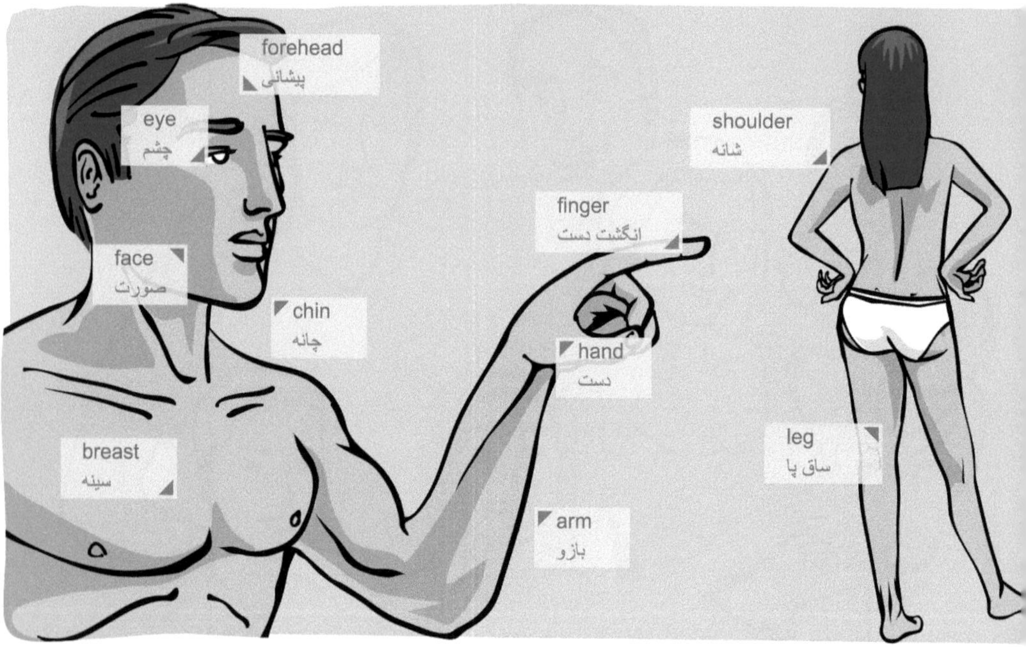

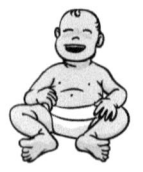

baby
کودک

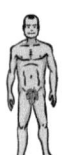

man
مرد

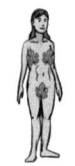

woman
زن

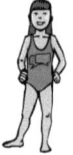

girl
دختربچه

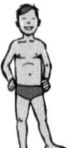

boy
پسربچه

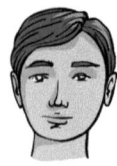

head
کله

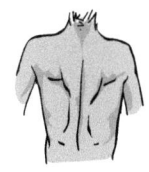

back

کمر

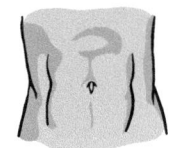

belly

شکم

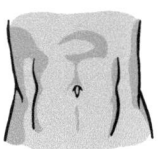

navel

ناف

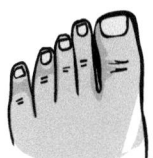

toe

انگشت پا

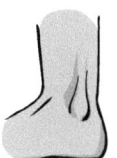

heel

پاشنه

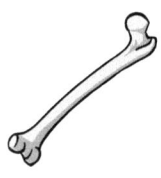

bone

استخوان

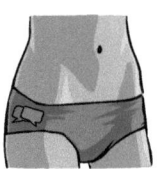

hip

لگن

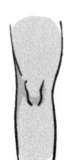

knee

زانو

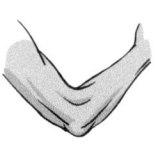

elbow

آرنج

nose

بینی

buttocks

نشیمنگاه

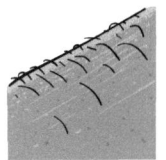

skin

پوست

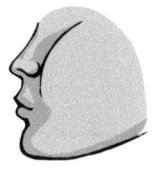

cheek

گونه

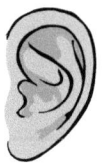

ear

گوش

lip

لب

mouth

دهان

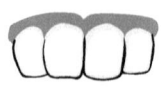

tooth

دندان

tongue

زبان

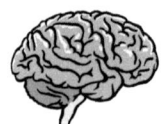

brain

مغز

heart

قلب

muscle

عضله

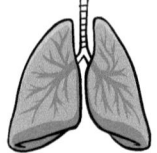

lung

ریه

liver

کبد

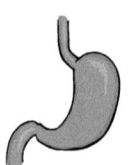

stomach

معده

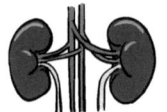

kidneys

کلیه

sex

آمیزش جنسی

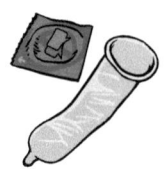

condom

کاندوم

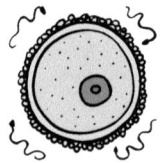

ovum

تخمک

semen

اسپرم

pregnancy

حاملگی

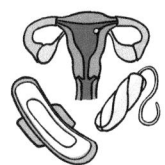

menstruation

پریود

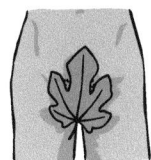

vagina

واژن

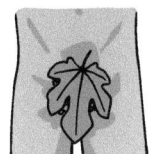

penis

آلت تناسلی مرد

eyebrow

ابرو

hair

مو

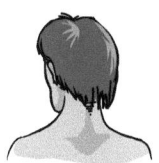

neck

گردن

hospital

بیمارستان

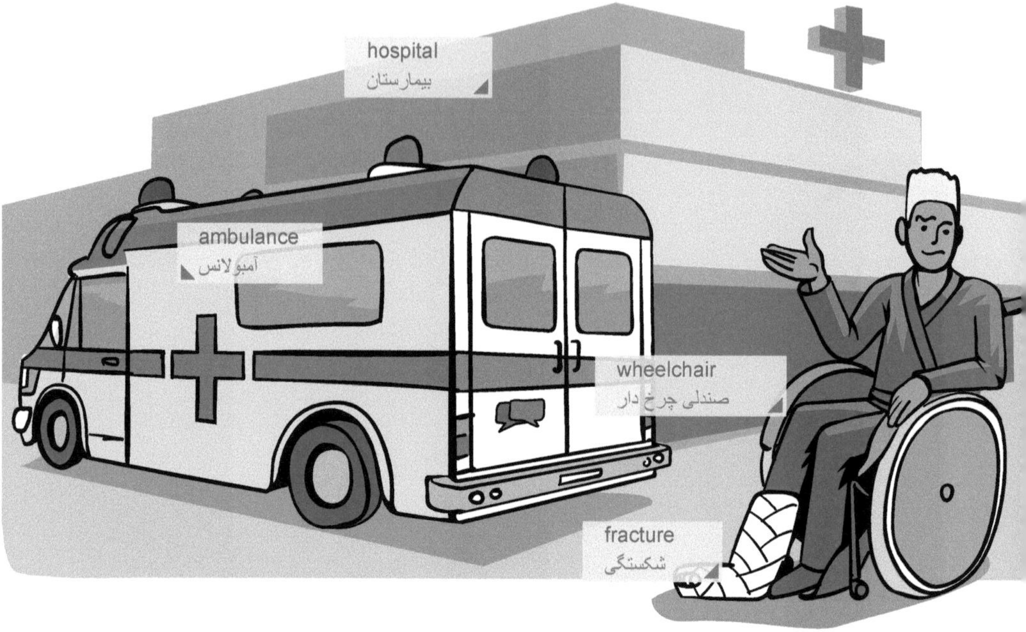

hospital
بیمارستان
ambulance
آمبولانس
wheelchair
صندلی چرخ دار
fracture
شکستگی

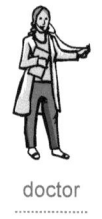

doctor

دکتر

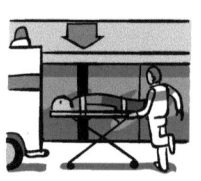

emergency room

بخش اورژانس

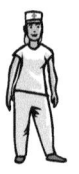

nurse

پرستار

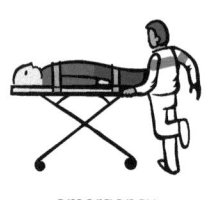

emergency

موقعیت اضطراری

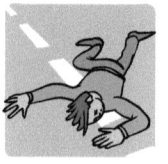

unconscious

بی هوش

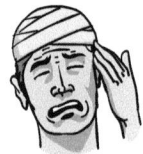

pain

درد

injury

مصدومیت

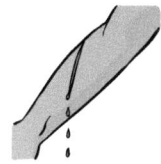

bleeding

خونریزی

heart attack

سکته قلبی

stroke

سکته مغزی

allergy

آلرژی

cough

سرفه

fever

تب

flu

آنفولانزا

diarrhea

اسهال

headache

سردرد

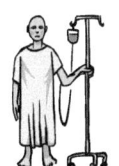

cancer

سرطان

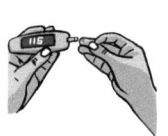

diabetes

دیابت

surgeon

جراح

scalpel

چاقوی جراحی

operation

عمل جراحی

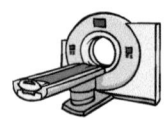

CT

سی تی اسکن

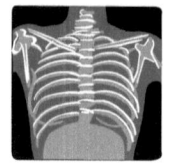

x-ray

پرتونگاری

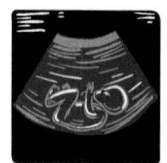

ultrasound

سونوگرافی

face mask

ماسک صورت

disease

بیماری

waiting room

اتاق انتظار

crutch

چوب زیر بغل

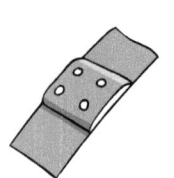

plaster

چسب زخم

bandage

پانسمان

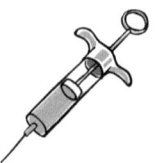

injection

تزریق

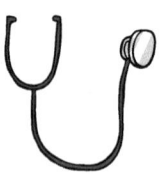

stethoscope

گوشی طبی

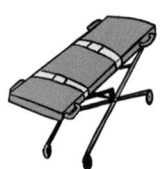

stretcher

برانکار

clinical thermometer

دماسنج

birth

زایش

overweight

اضافه وزن

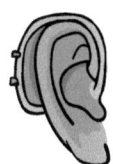

hearing aid

سمعک

disinfectant

ماده ضد غفونی کننده

infection

عفونت

virus

ویروس

HIV / AIDS

اچ ای وی / ایدز

medicine

دارو

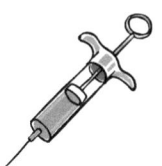

vaccination

واکسیناسیون

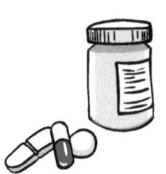

tablets

قرص

pill

قرص ضد حاملگی

emergency call

تماس اظطراری

blood pressure monitor

دستگاه اندازه گیری فشارخون

ill / healthy

مریض / سالم

Help!

کمک!

alarm

آژیر خطر

assault

حمله

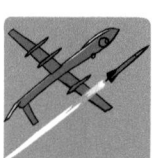

attack

حمله ی فیزیکی

danger

خطر

emergency exit

خروج اظطراری

Fire!

آتش

fire extinguisher

کپسول آتش نشانی

accident

تصادف

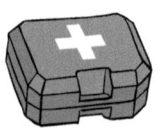

first-aid kit

جعبه کمک های اولیه

SOS

درخواست کمک

police

پلیس

Europe

اروپا

North America

آمریکای شمالی

South America

آمریکای جنوبی

Africa

آفریقا

Asia

آسیا

Australia

استرالیا

Atlantic

اقیا نوس اطلس

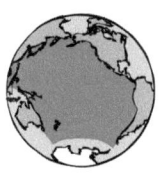

Pacific

اقیانوس آرام

Indian Ocean

اقیانوس هند

Antarctic Ocean

اقیا نوس اطلس جنوبی

Arctic Ocean

اقیانوس منجمد شمالی

North pole

قطب شمال

South pole

قطب جنوب

Antarctica

قاره قطب جنوب

earth

کره زمین

land

سرزمین

sea

دریا

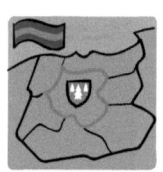

island

جزیره

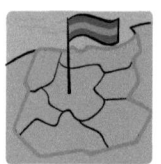

nation

ملت

state

کشور

clock face

صفحه ی ساعت

hour hand

ساعت شمار

minute hand

دقیقه شمار

second hand

ثانیه شمار

What time is it?

ساعت چند است؟

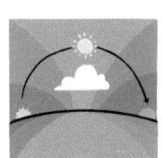

day

روز

time

زمان

now

اکنون

digital watch

ساعت دیجیتال

minute

دقیقه

hour

ساعت

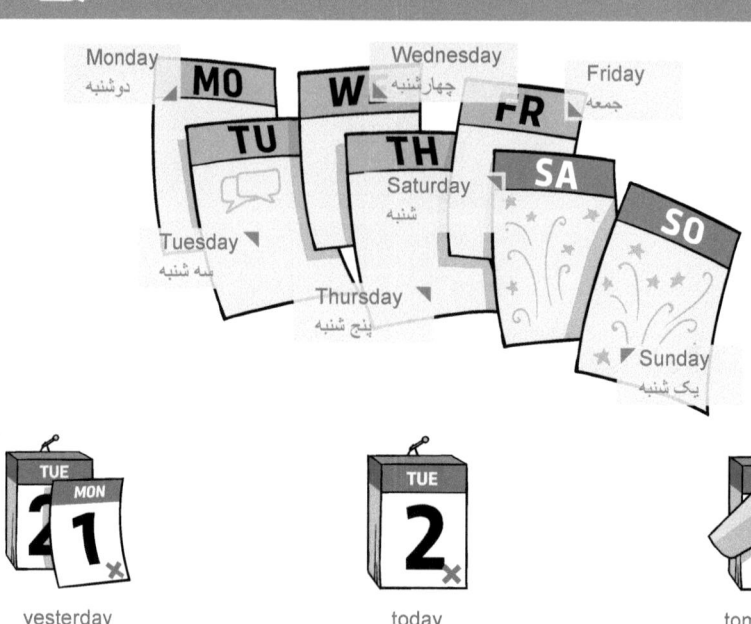

Monday
دوشنبه

Wednesday
چهارشنبه

Friday
جمعه

Saturday
شنبه

Tuesday
سه شنبه

Thursday
پنج شنبه

Sunday
یک شنبه

yesterday
....
دیروز

today
....
امروز

tomorrow
....
فردا

morning
....
صبح

noon
....
ظهر

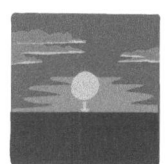

evening
....
غروب

workdays
....
روزهای کاری

weekend
....
آخر هفته

year

سال

rain
باران
snow
برف
wind
باد
spring
بهار
summer
تابستان
fall
پاییز
winter
زمستان

4.APRIL 11°
5.APRIL 4°
6.APRIL 13°
7.APRIL 8°
8.APRIL 10°

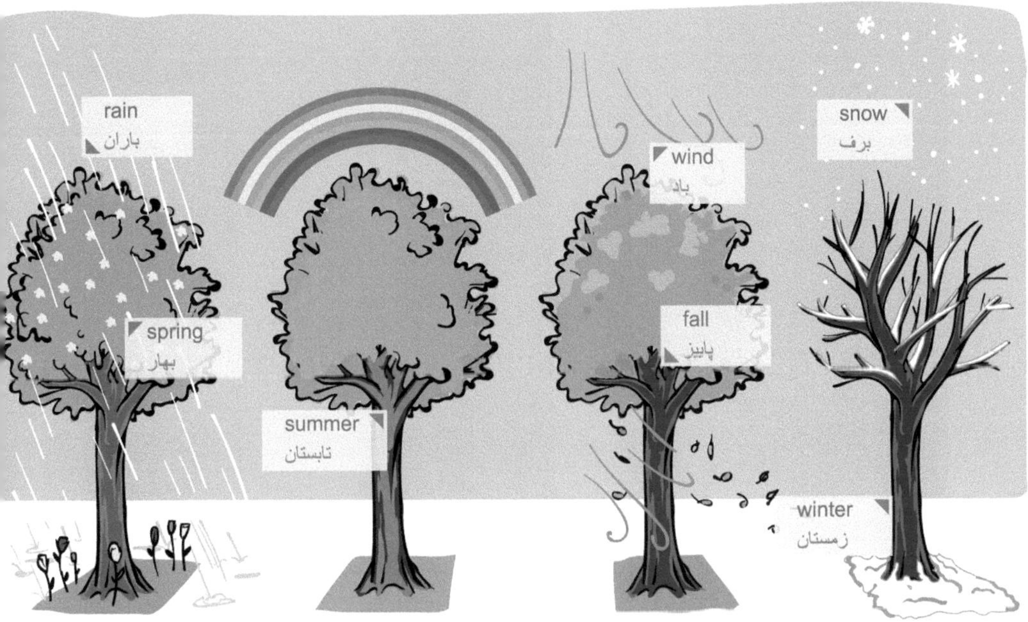

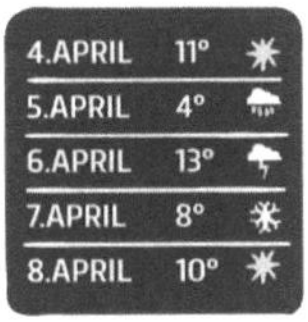

weather forecast

پیش‌بینی اوضاع جوی

F C
120 40
90 30
60 20
30 10
0 0
-30 -10
-20

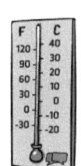

thermometer

دماسنج

sunshine

تابش آفتاب

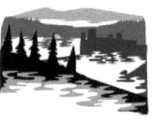

cloud

ابر

fog

مه

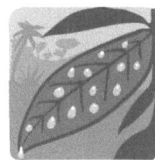

humidity

رطوبت هوا

lightning

صاعقه

thunder

آسمان غره

storm

طوفان

hail

تگرگ

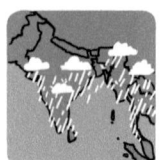

monsoon

باد موسمی

flood

سیل

ice

یخ

January

ژانویه

February

فوریه

March

مارس

April

آوریل

May

مه

June

ژوئن

July

ژوئیه

August

آگوست

September

سپتامبر

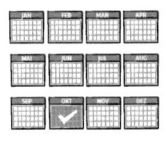

October

اکتبر

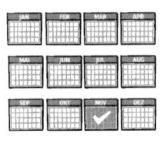

November

نوامبر

December

دسامبر

shapes

أشكال

circle

دايره

square

مربع

rectangle

مستطيل

triangle

سه گوش

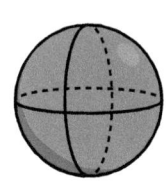

sphere

گره

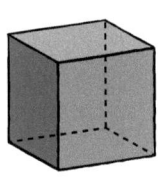

cube

مكعب مربع

white

سفید

yellow

زرد

orange

نارنجی

pink

صورتی

red

قرمز

purple

بنفش

blue

آبی

green

سبز

brown

قهوه ای

gray

خاکستری

black

سیاه

a lot / a little

خیلی / کم

angry / calm

خشمگین / آرام

beautiful / ugly

زیبا / زشت

beginning / end

شروع / پایان

big / small

بزرگ / کوچک

bright / dark

روشن / تیره

brother / sister

برادر / خواهر

clean / dirty

تمیز / آلوده

complete / incomplete

کامل / ناقص

day / night

روز / شب

dead / alive

مرده / زنده

wide / narrow

پهن / باریک

edible / inedible

قابل خوردن / غیر قابل خوردن

evil / kind

غضبناک / مهربان

excited / bored

هیجان زده / بی حوصله

fat / thin

چاق / لاغر

first / last

اولین / آخرین

friend / enemy

دوست / دشمن

full / empty

پر / خالی

hard / soft

سفت / نرم

heavy / light

سنگین / سبک

hunger / thirst

گرسنگی / تشنگی

ill / healthy

مریض / سالم

illegal / legal

غیرقانونی / قانونی

intelligent / stupid

باهوش / خنگ

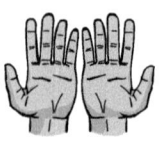

left / right

چپ / راست

near / far

نزدیک / دور

opposites - متضاد ها

new / used

نو / استفاده شده

nothing / something

هیچ چیز / چیزی

old / young

پیر / جوان

on / off

روشن / خاموش

open / closed

باز / بسته

quiet / loud

آهسته / بلند

rich / poor

ثروتمند / فقیر

right / wrong

درست / غلط

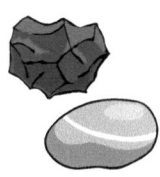

rough / smooth

زبر / صاف

sad / happy

غمگین / خوشحال

short / long

کوتاه / بلند

slow / fast

کند / تند

wet / dry

تر / خشک

warm / cool

گرم / خنک

war / peace

جنگ / صلح

0	**1**	**2**
zero	one	two
صفر	یک	دو

3	**4**	**5**
three	four	five
سه	چهار	پنج

6	**7**	**8**
six	seven	eight
شش	هفت	هشت

9	**10**	**11**
nine	ten	eleven
نه	ده	یازده

12

twelve

دوازده

13

thirteen

سیزده

14

fourteen

چهارده

15

fifteen

پانزده

16

sixteen

شانزده

17

seventeen

هفده

18

eighteen

هجده

19

nineteen

نوزده

20

twenty

بیست

100

hundred

صد

1.000

thousand

هزار

1.000.000

million

میلیون

languages

زبان ها

English

انگلیسی

American English

انگلیسی آمریکایی

Chinese Mandarin

چینی ماندارین

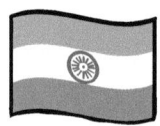

Hindi

هندی

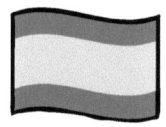

Spanish

اسپانیایی

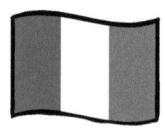

French

فرانسوی

Arabic

عربی

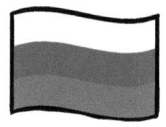

Russian

روسی

Portuguese

پرتغالی

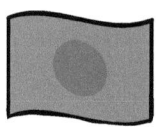

Bengali

بنگالی

German

آلمانی

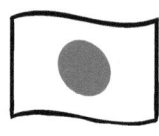

Japanese

ژاپنی

I

من

you

تو

he / she / it

او

we

ما

you

شما

they

أنها

who?

چه کسی؟ کی؟

what?

چی؟

how?

چگونه؟

where?

کجا؟

when?

کی؟

name

نام

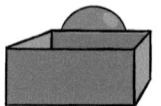

behind

پشت

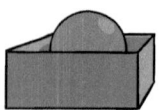

in

توی

in front of

جلو

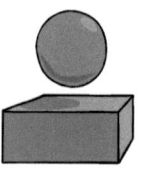

over

بالای

on

روی

under

زیر

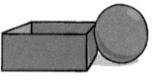

beside

مجاور

between

بین

place

مکان